To Toby With Love

From Grandad

Barbel

1986.

FISHING STEP BY STEP

Barbel

with

Pete Frost

CASSELL
LONDON

CASSELL & COMPANY LIMITED
35 Red Lion Square, London WC1R 4SG
and at Sydney, Auckland, Toronto, Johannesburg,
an affiliate of
Macmillan Publishing Co., Inc.,
New York.

First published 1976

ISBN 0 304 29750 X

Printed by Ian Allan Printing Ltd.

INTRODUCTION

If you can put a rod together, use a reel and handle a landing net, then these books are your next need. With this series of books the angler is given the chance of seeing just how the expert goes about catching the fish that have made his name a household word in the world of fishing.

Peter Mohan has used his unique knowledge of angling personalities to select the right angler for each book, and then edited the series as a whole.

Ken Whitehead has spent days at the water with the experts, patiently filming and planning every photograph so that each picture shows in detail where, when and how the many tasks are approached.

Study the pictures and compare your methods, your tackle and your whole approach to fishing. This is how you will gain the confidence that brings success.

Whilst the books in themselves are interesting to read, they are also a programmed technique that is progressive. With careful study the new angler, or one wishing to improve his angling will learn how each skill at the water should be tackled, and by re-reading he will be able to adopt the expert's way of tackling every situation.

1 Just the place for a barbel! Weir pools are typical barbel swims.

2 Gravel lies likely to hold barbel can easily be spotted if you wear polaroid sunglasses to cut out the light.

3

4

3 The author's 12ft three-piece glass trotting rod; excellent for use with a line of about 5lb breaking strain.

4 An 11ft 6in glass rod used with the swing tip shown for ledgering in waters where the current is not strong.

5 Shorter two-piece rod for lines of 6-10lb breaking strain for use in strong currents or where larger fish are expected.

6 The popular Mitchell 300 reel.

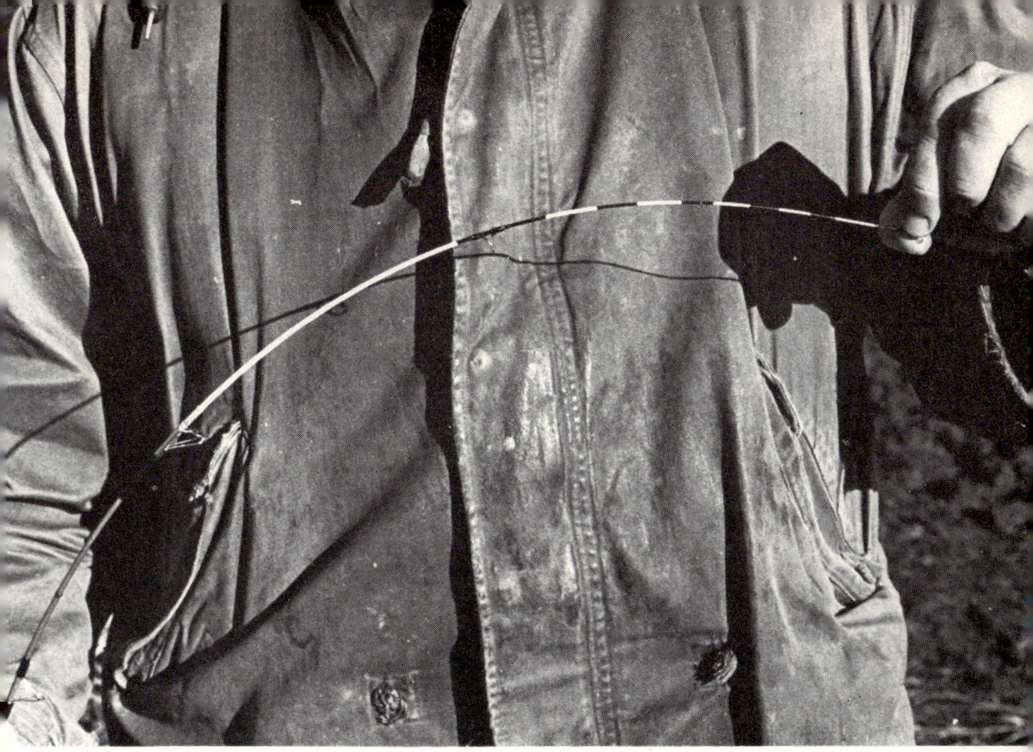

7 Little used by anglers today, the centre pin reel is still favoured by experts for its good line control when trotting.

8 More sensitive than the swing tip, the quiver tip shown here is an extension of the actual tip of the rod.

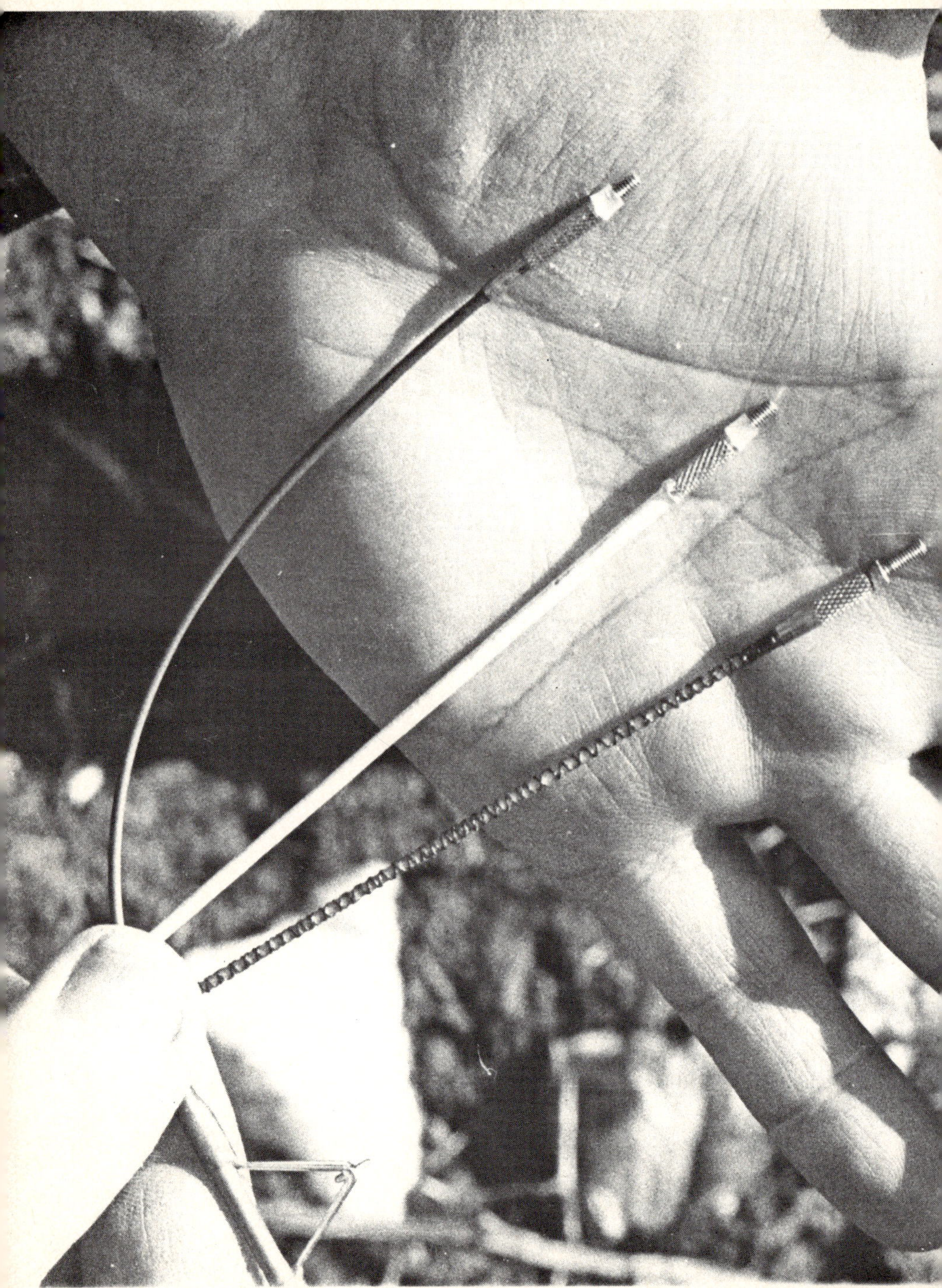

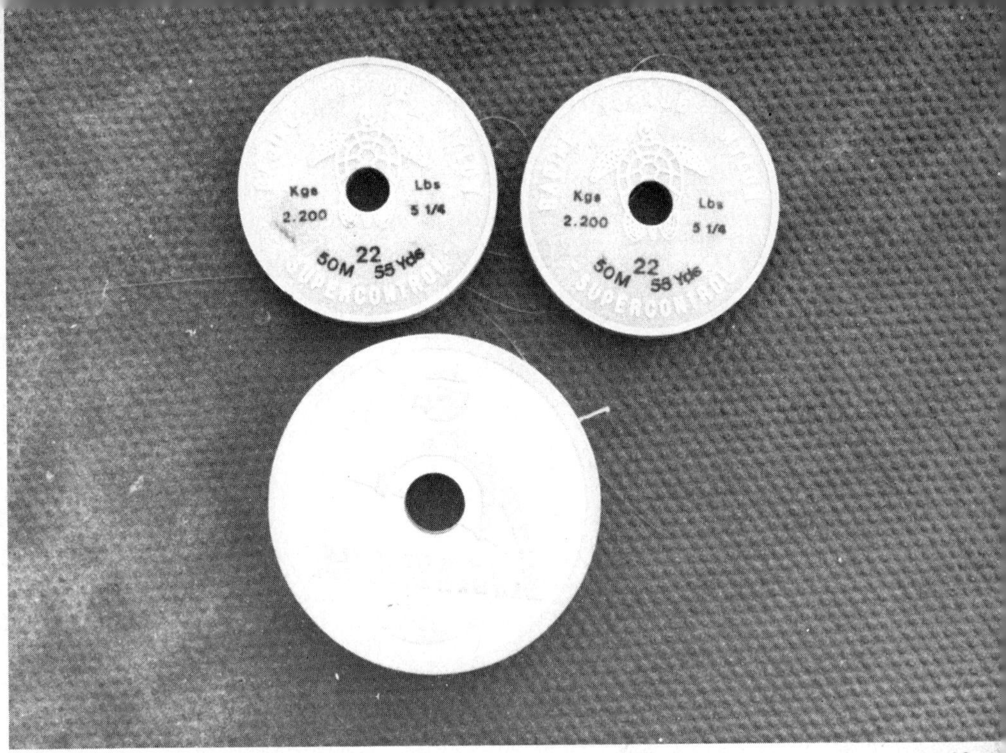

10

9 Swing tips often twist and fail to line up with the tip ring of the rod, so the author uses a plastic or rubber 'sleeve' which keeps the swing tip in position.

10 The author's favourite lines.

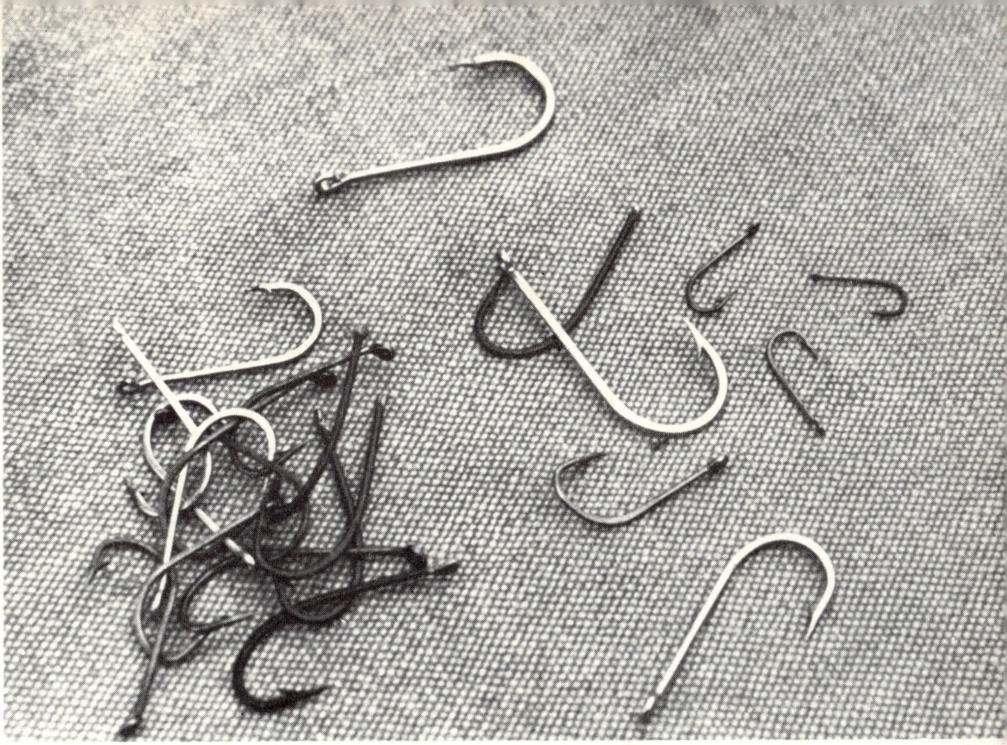

11 Arlesey bombs of different sizes; the best weights for ledgering.

12 A selection of hooks, all good for barbel fishing.

13

14

13 An open-ended swim feeder for distributing small amounts of groundbait around the hook baits.

14 Block feeder and cone feeder for ground-baiting with maggots.

15 The bait dropper; yet another method of depositing maggots on the bottom, but this time for use in swims where the current runs swiftly.

16

16 Float selection.

17 The author prefers a circular landing net so that fish can be brought into the net from any direction.

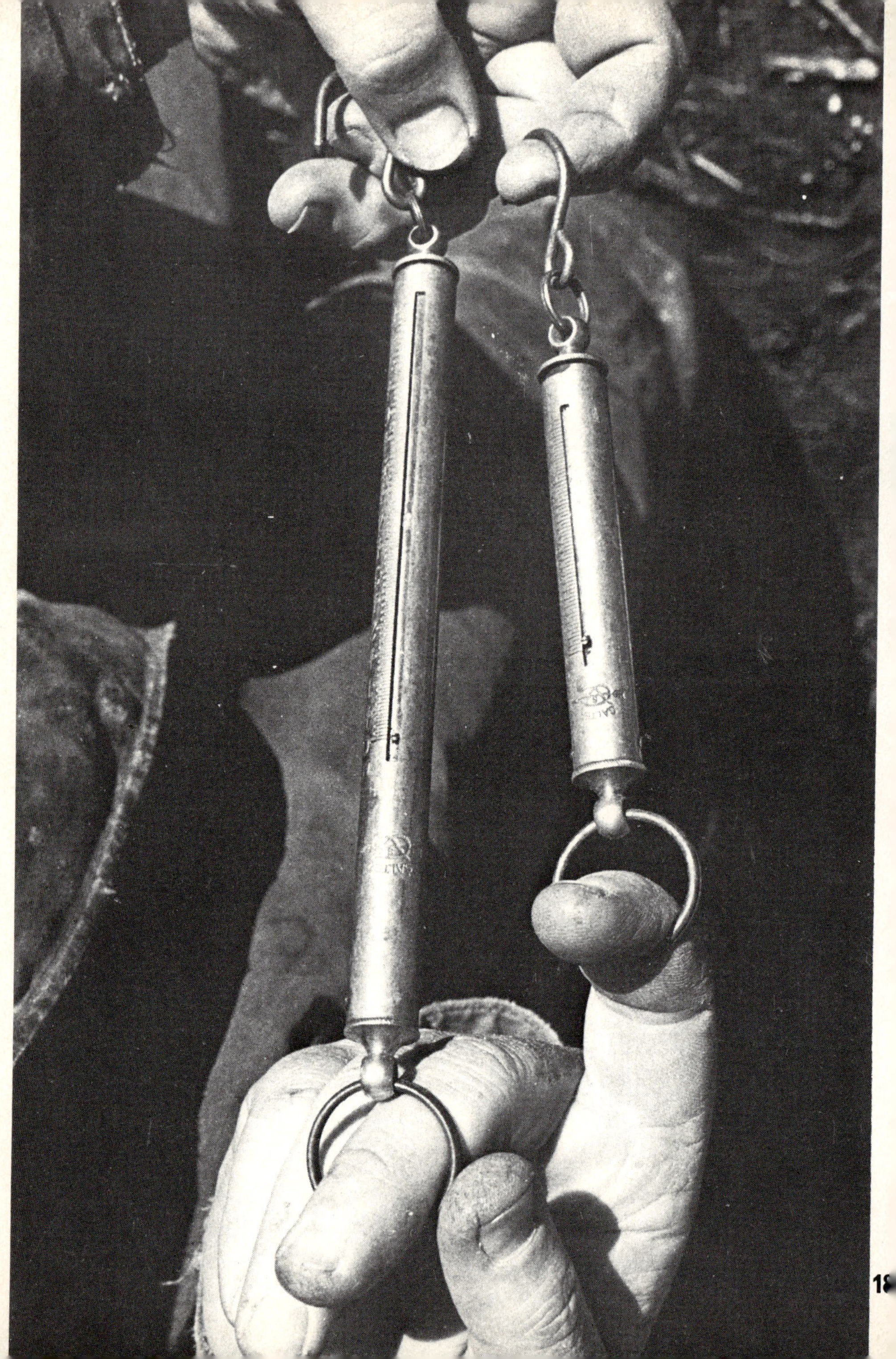

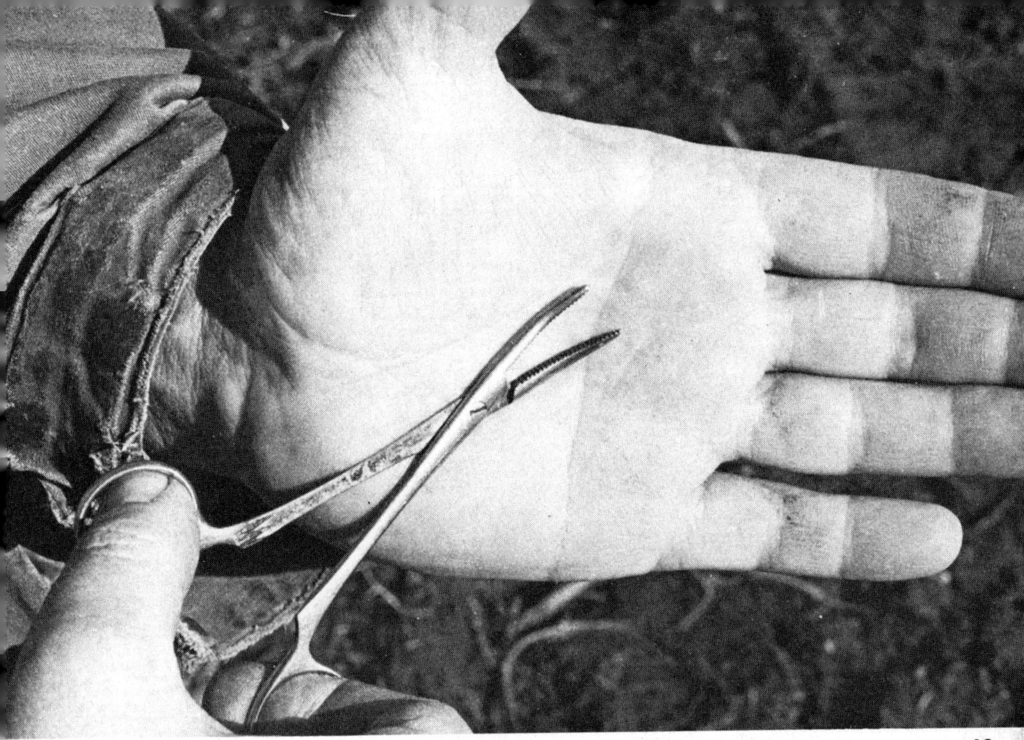

18 Spring balances — easy to carry and fairly accurate.

19 Artery forceps — better for extracting hooks than the old type of disgorger.

20

21

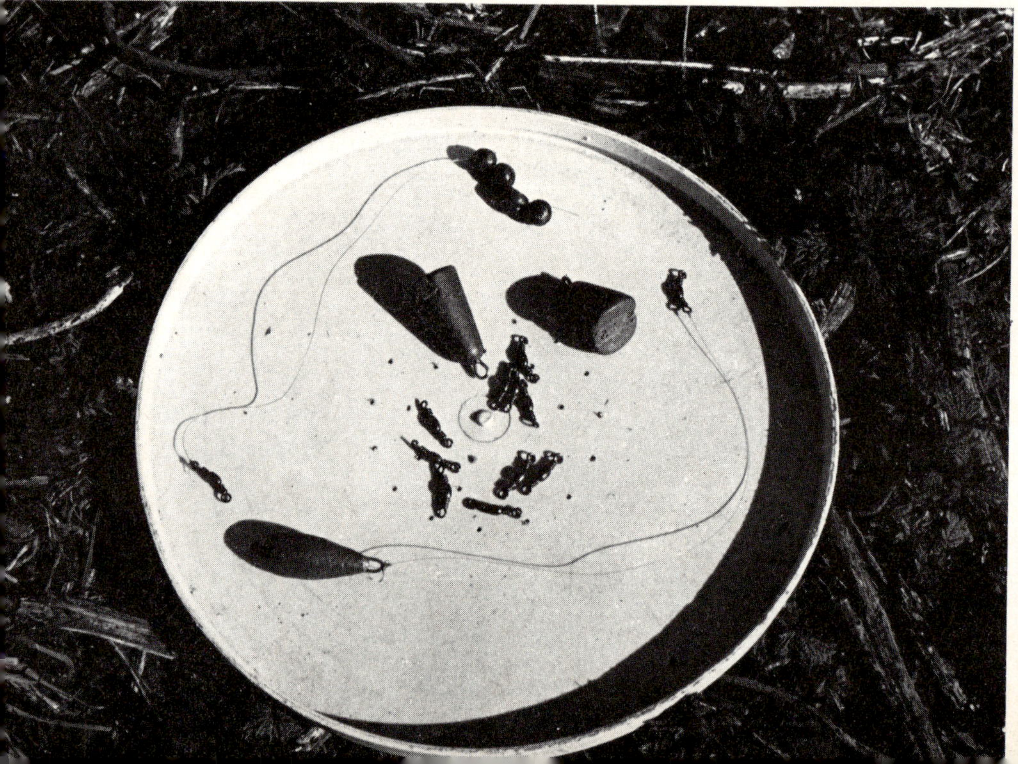

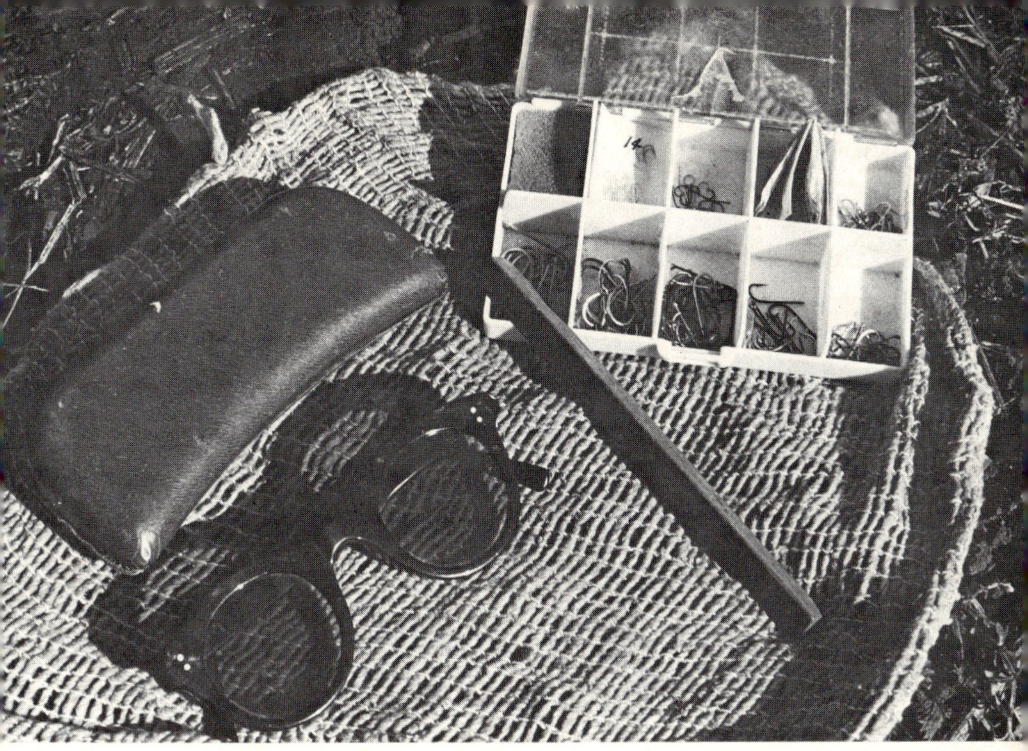

22

20 Split shot weights and a selection of float caps.

21 Plummets are useful for depth finding, and swivels have many uses, such as attaching the link ledger shown to the reel line.

22 Most hooks need sharpening, so keep a sharpening stone in your tackle box. The usefulness of polaroid sunglasses has already been mentioned.

23

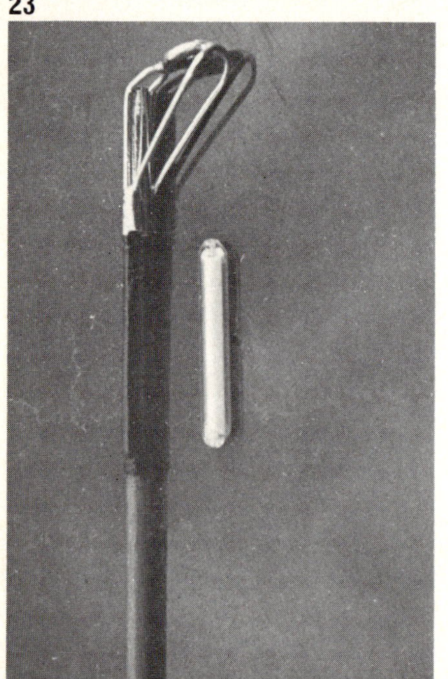

24

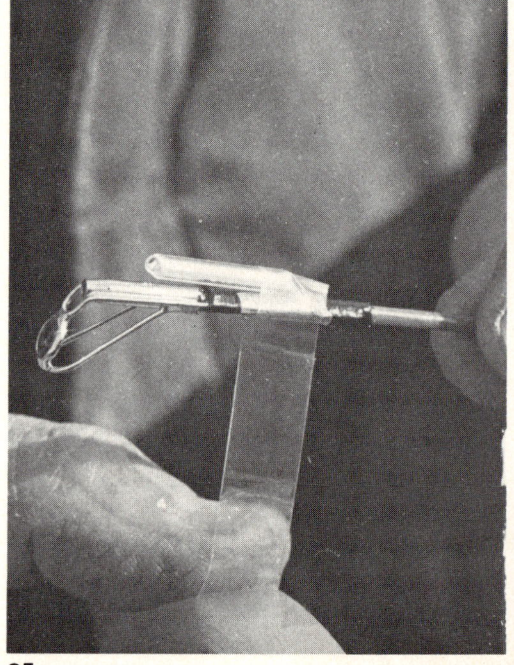

25

26

23 The seat box is reasonably comfortable, and it holds most of the tackle required.

24 A Betalight; a gas-filled light source which lasts some 20 years.

25 Attached to the rod tip for short night-fishing sessions, the Betalight makes it easy to see bites.

26 A small but important point so often forgotten by anglers is to keep the spool filled almost to the lip with line for longer and more accurate casting.

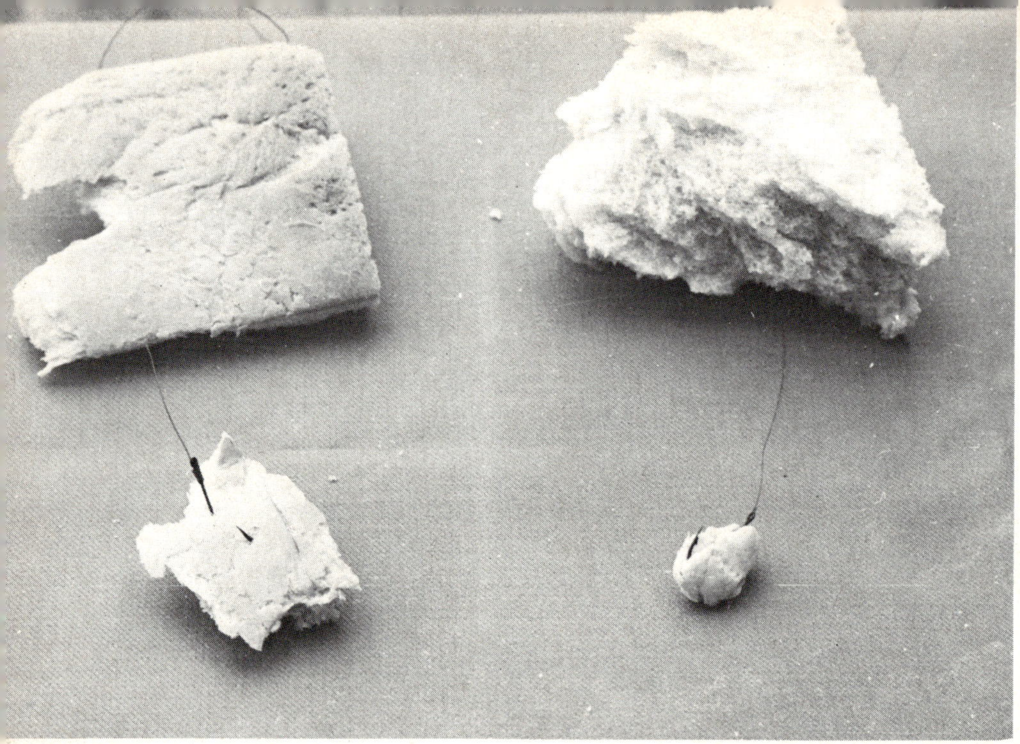

27

28

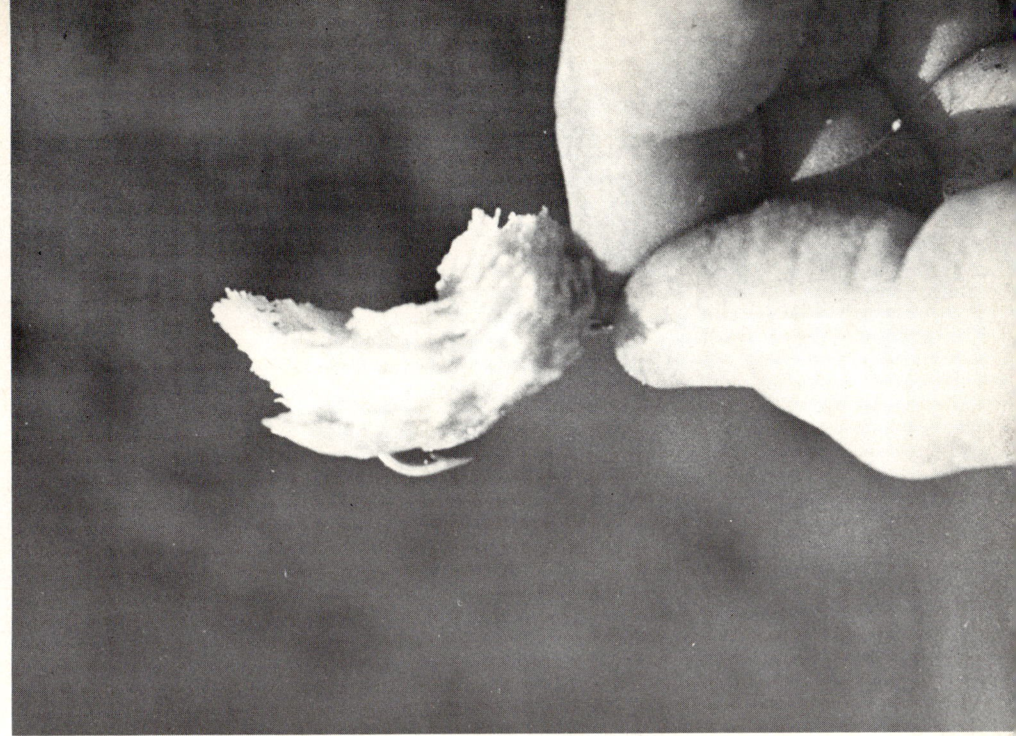

27 Still one of the best baits!

28 The best way to put the crust on the hook.

29 Bread flake — the inside of the loaf — pinched onto the hook, leaving the point and barb showing for easy penetration.

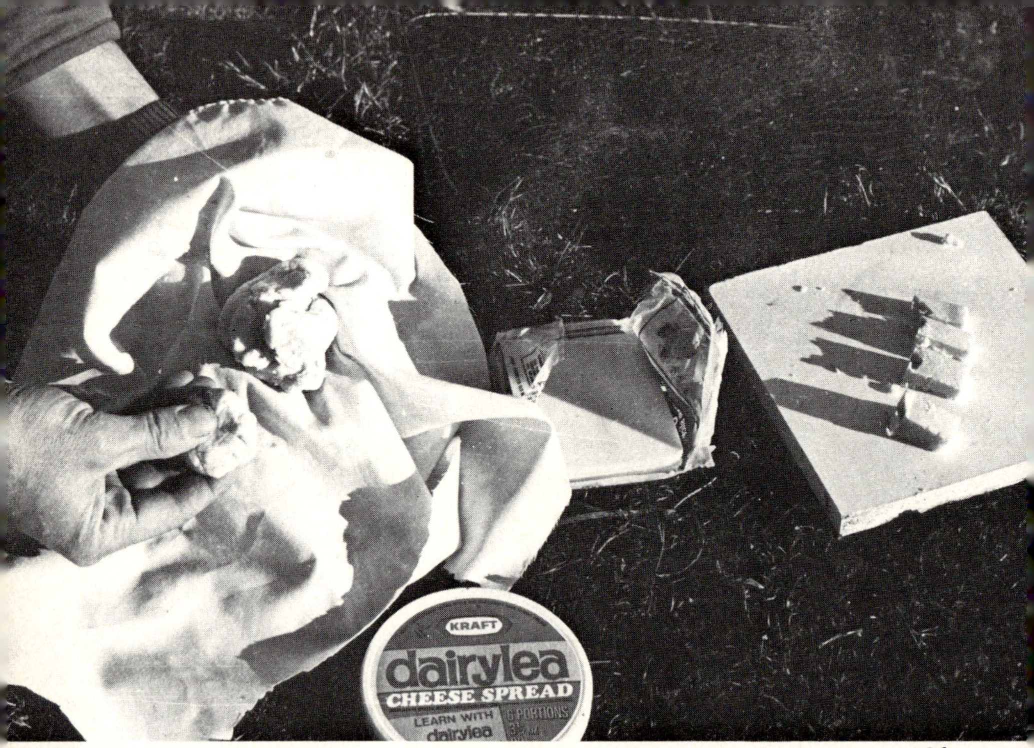

30

31

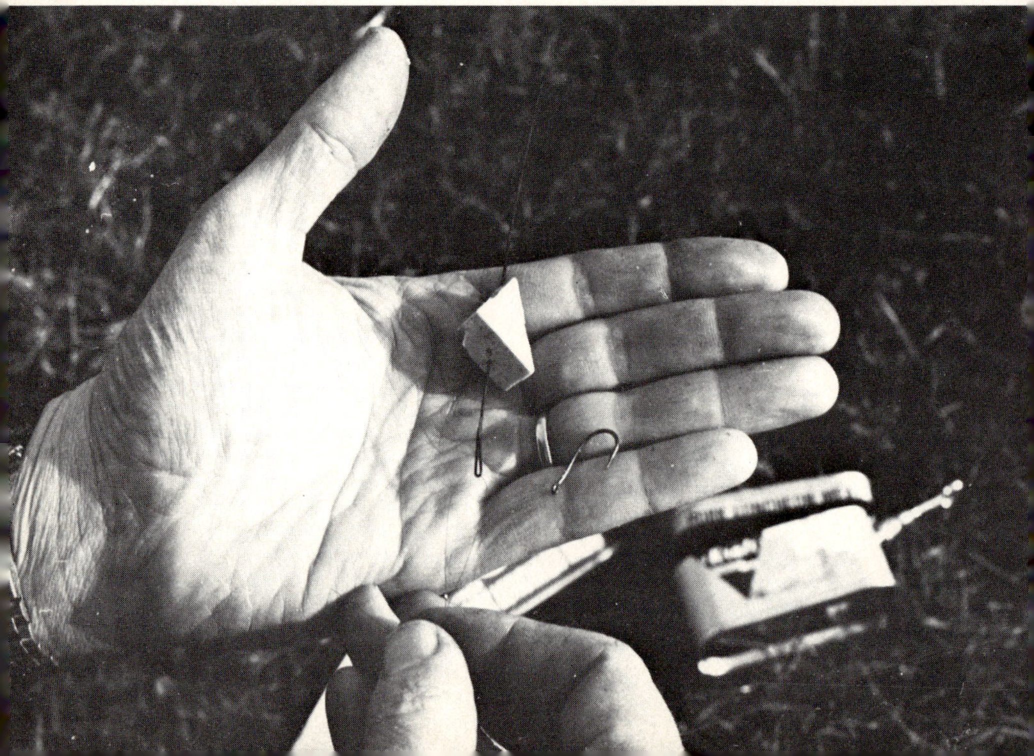

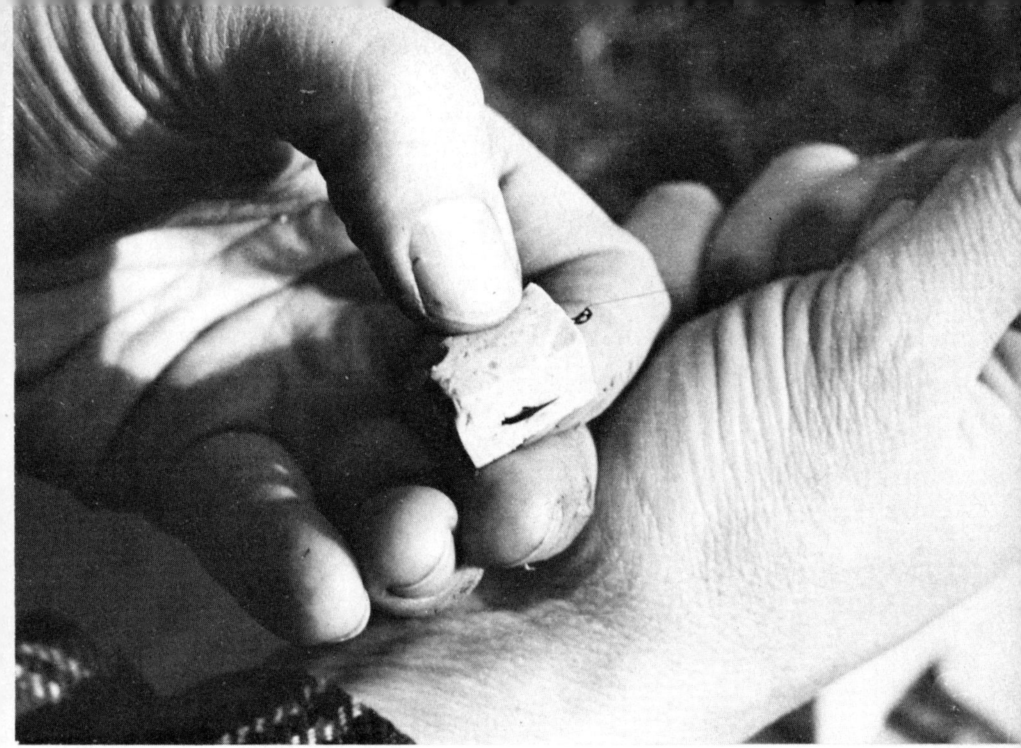

32

30 Mixing cheese and bread for cheese paste.

31 Barbel like meat, especially luncheon meat.

32 Hooking luncheon meat.

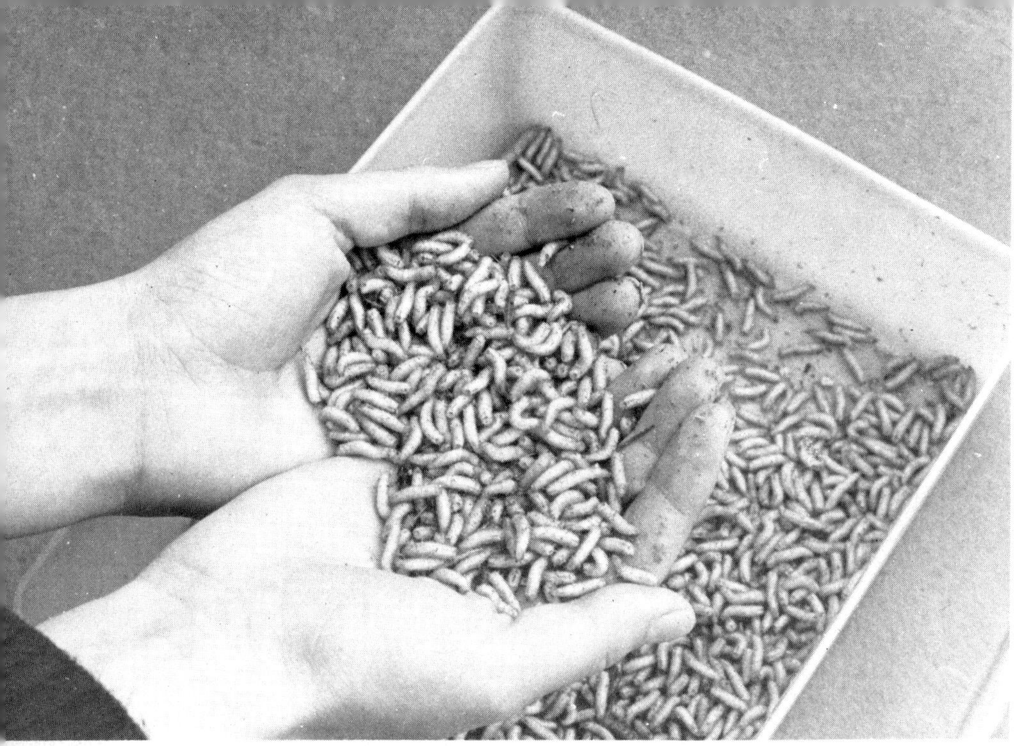

33

33 Maggots — a very good barbel bait on many waters, though banned on the lower Hampshire Avon!

34 Casters. This is the first stage change from the maggot, light brown to orange in colour. Casters can be held at this stage for a while in a refrigerator, and placed in water they should sink. If they have 'gone' too far they float and are dark brown in colour.

34

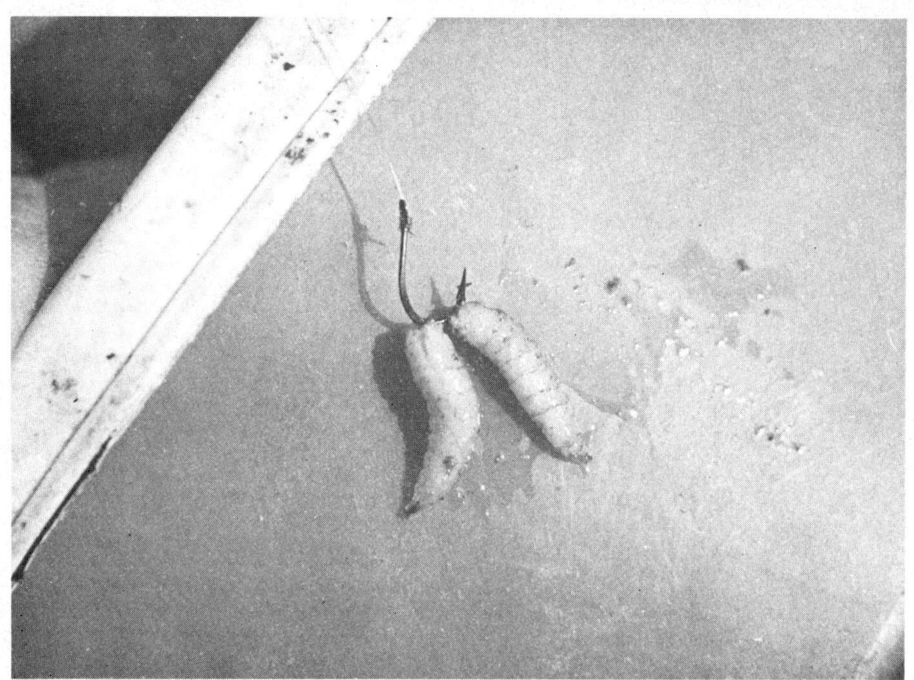

35

35 The right way to put a maggot on the hook.

36 Sausage meat is another good bait, but it needs to be stiffened with breadcrumbs or groundbait to make a good paste.

38

37 Hempseed — an excellent bait, but banned on some waters. The seed should be allowed to simmer until the grain splits.

38 Bacon and liver — often good baits for large and 'difficult' fish.

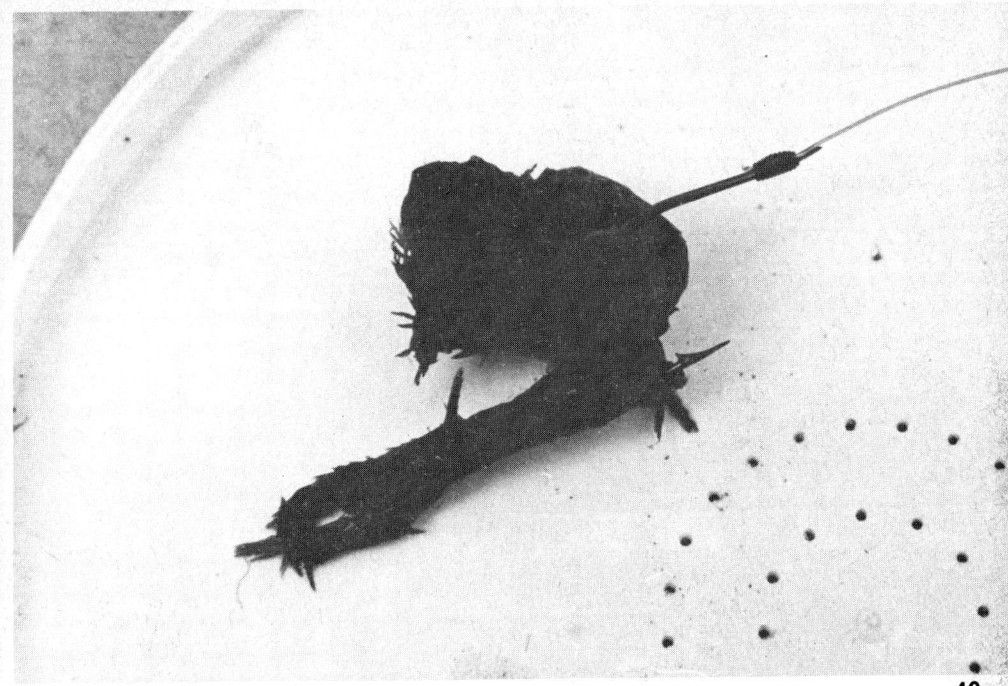

40

39 Silkweed, a dark green, slimy weed which often grows on weir sills where barbel feed in the early part of the season.

40 The silkweed can be wrapped round the hook, although it is sometimes possible to get enough simply by dragging a hook through the growing weed.

41

41 A 'carp-type' special, in this case Kit-e-Kat and sausage meat paste.

42 A natural bait, the freshwater swan mussel, found almost buried in mud or silt, often near reeds.

43

43 Hook the inside of the mussel through the toughest part.

44

44 To open, insert a knife blade and cut the muscle at each end of the shell.

45

46

45 A small fish, alive or dead, such as this bleak, is an excellent bait for the barbel.

46 The flat-tailed lobworm is also a favourite with barbel.

47 Hook the worm like this.

48

48 The crayfish, found only in clear, pure waters. A large hook should be inserted underneath near the tail segment.

49 A flake and maggot 'cocktail', often taken when either bait alone would fail!

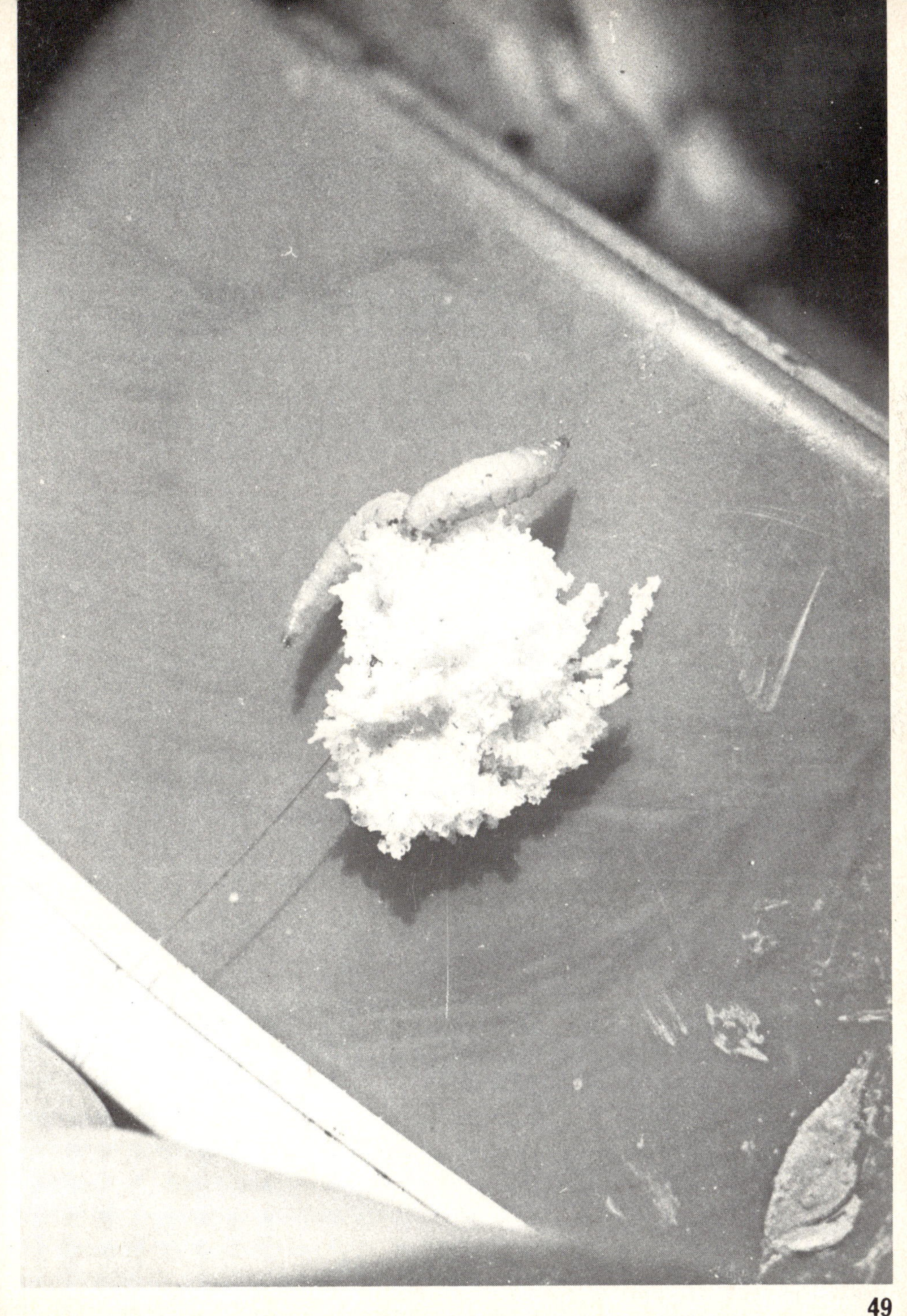

50 Preparing a crust bait by the Hilton 'carrot' method for finicky biters.

51 The largest piece is threaded onto the line first, and the smallest piece last.

52

Ledgering — How to detect a bite

52 Watching the rod tip for bites at dusk, with the rod high against the skyline.

53 Once more the rod tip is watched, this time with the rod low, and held on a rest.

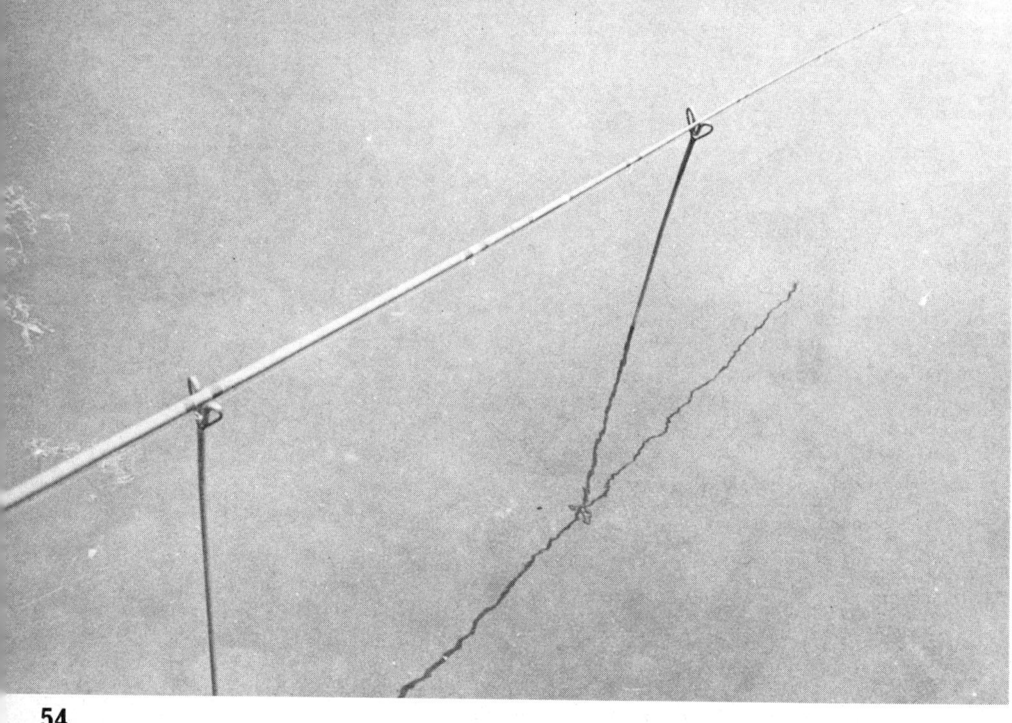

54

54 Here the author uses two 'front' rod rests to hold the tip still in high winds.

55 A more sensitive method of bite detection is shown here. The rod is held low on a rest, while the free hand 'feels' the line near the reel.

56

57

58

56 Upstream ledgering. As a fish lifts the bait, the line falls slack, and the bent rod tip will straighten. This is the time to strike.

57 The sensitive quiver tip in action.

58 A swing tip in use.

59

60

59 The author is slowly working the bait back towards him, feeling for bites at the same time.

Float fishing rigs

60 The 'Avon' type float.

61 A 'waggler' float.

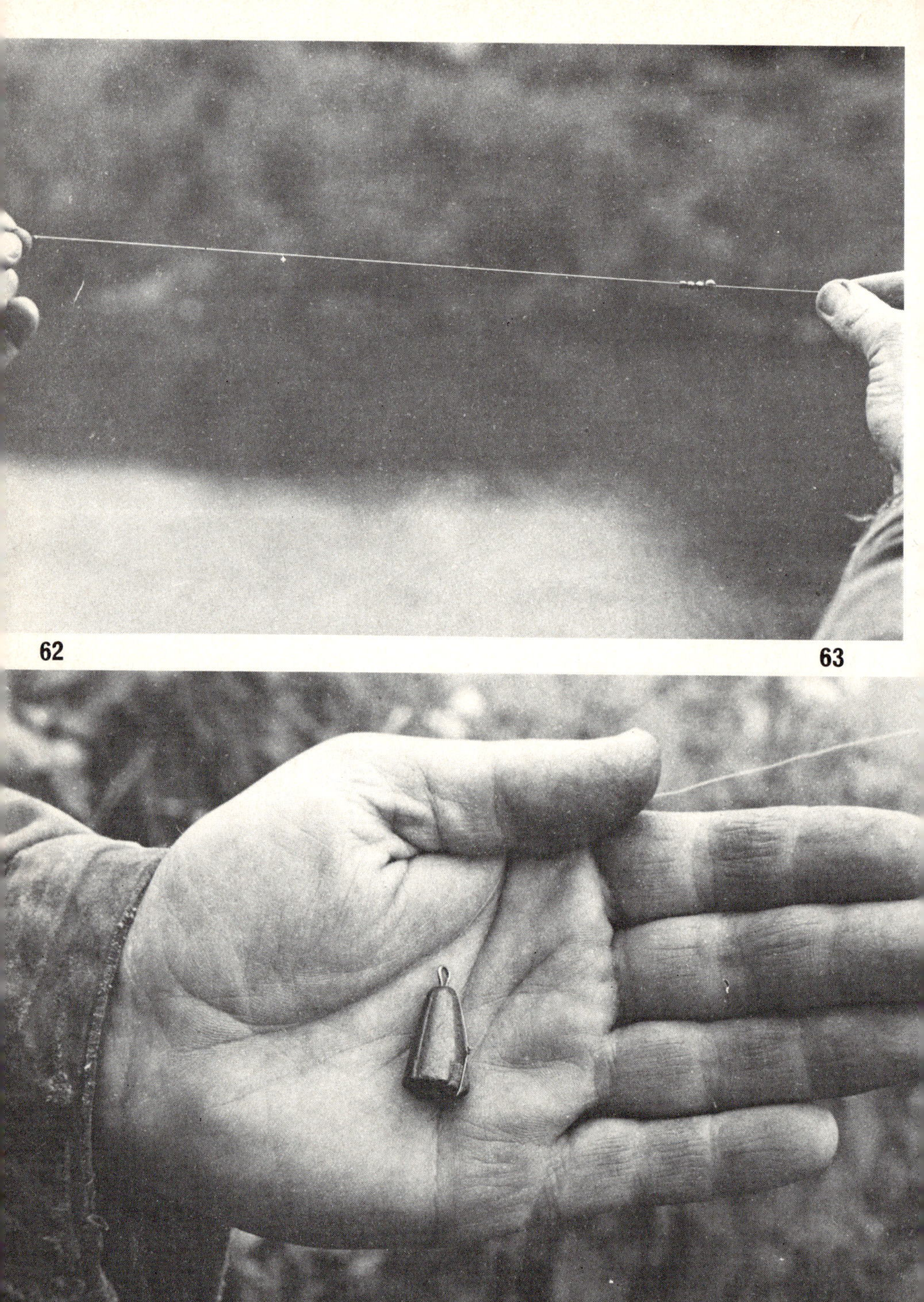
62

63

64

62 Shot bunched about fifteen inches from the hook — normal shotting for float fishing water four to five feet deep.

63 A plummet attached to the line.

64 Plumbing the depth.

65

66

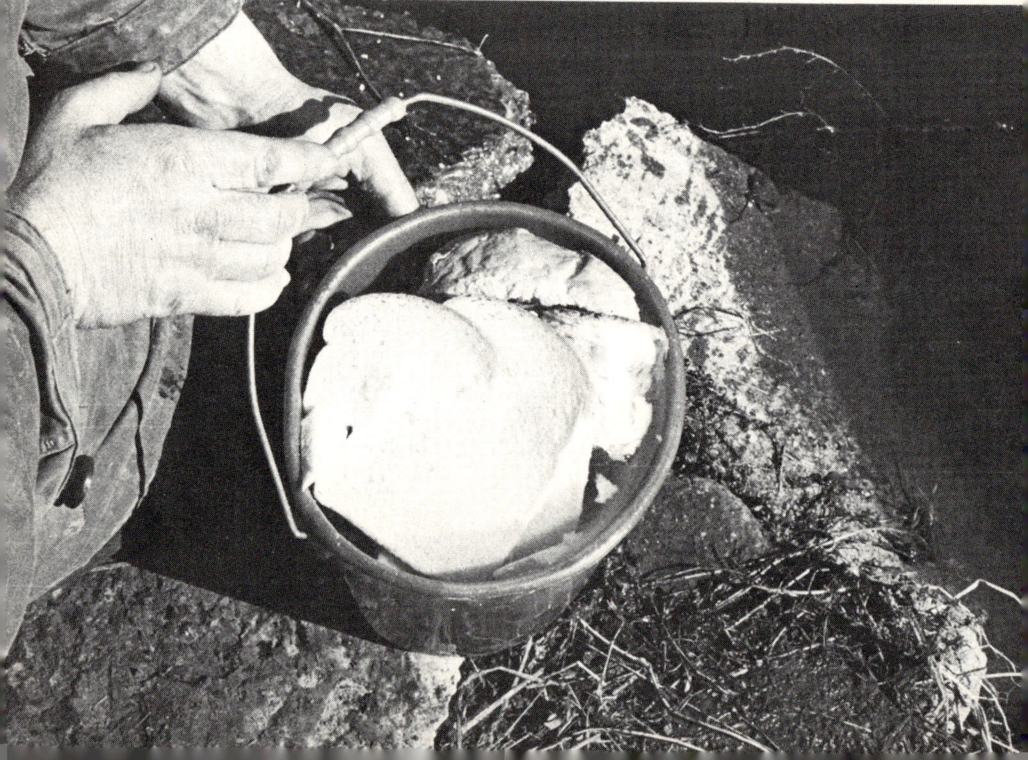

Groundbaiting

65 Throw the groundbait upstream, judging the speed of the flow so that it will reach the bottom where you intend to fish.

66 Soaking stale bread for use as groundbait.

67 Squeeze the groundbait as dry as possible to help it sink.

68

68 Mashing bread groundbait.

69 Added bran stiffens the bread and helps it to break up in water.

72

70 A stone will help to sink the groundbait more quickly in fast water.

71 A proprietary groundbait.

72 The swim feeder, sealed with groundbait.

74

73 Swim feeder loaded with maggots.

74 The block feeder.

75

76

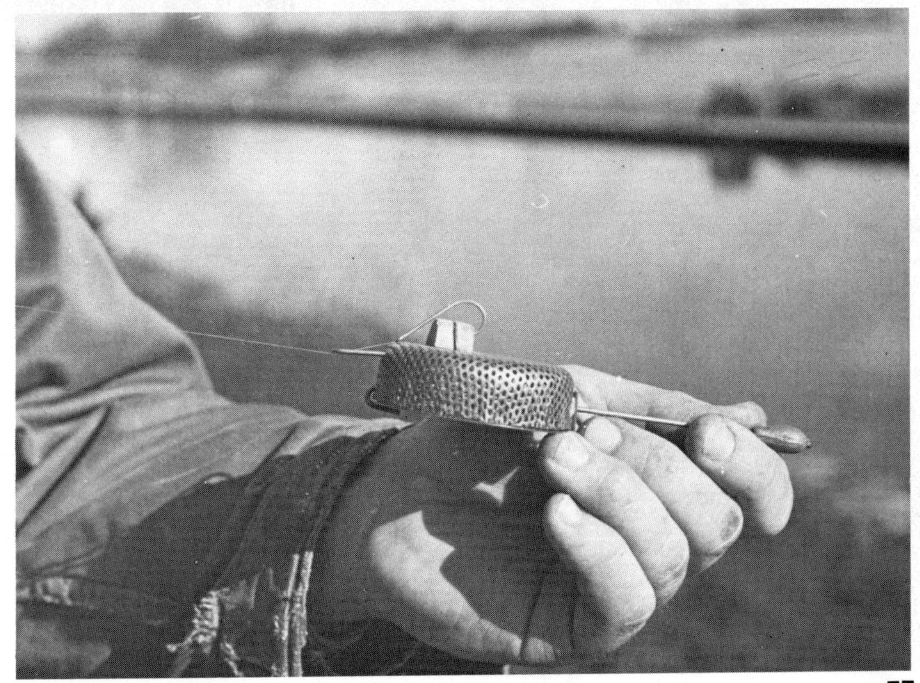

77

75 The best way to cast a loaded swim feeder. Swing the swim feeder back towards you . . .

76 . . . Then drive forward with the rod.

77 Attaching a bait dropper.

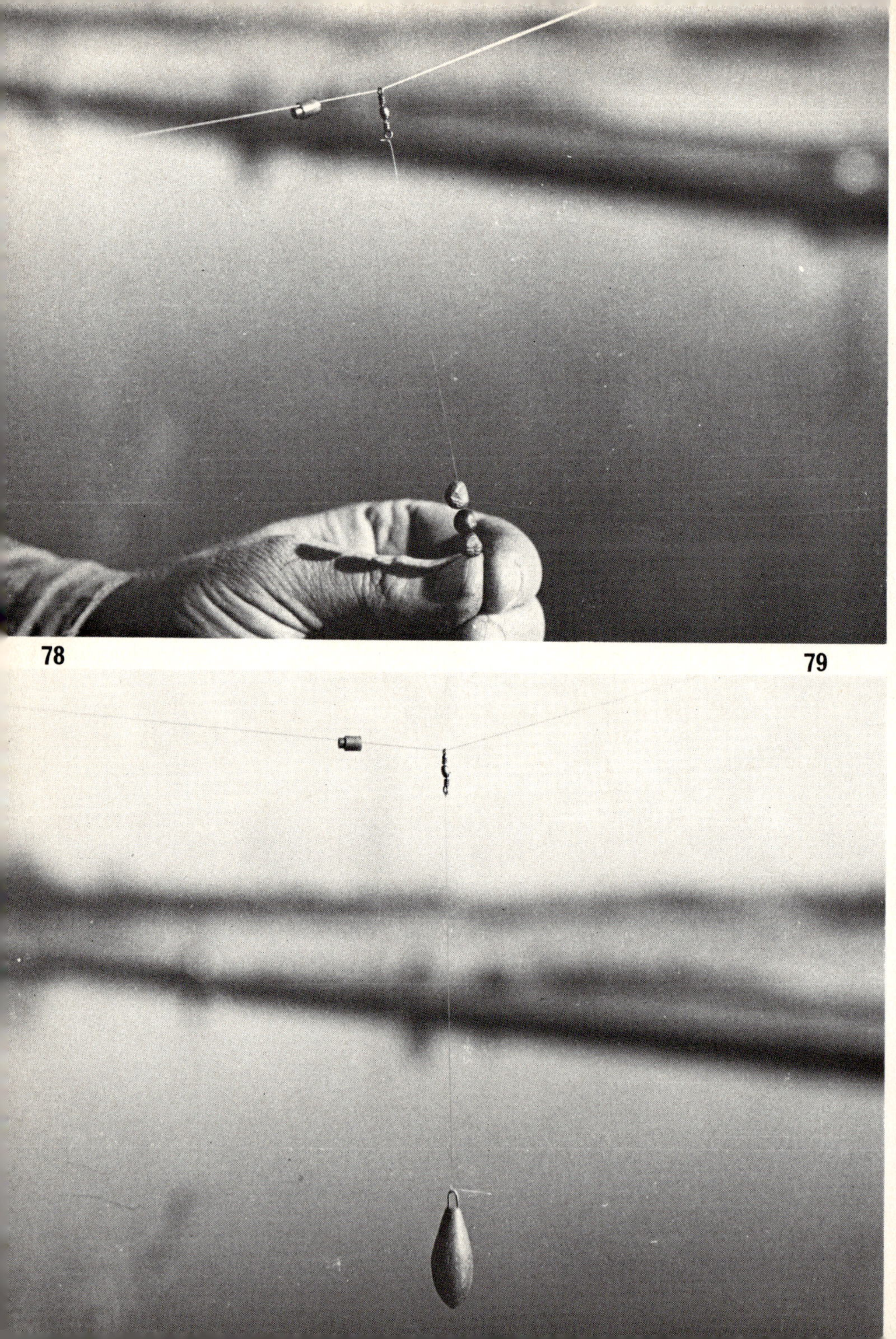

78

79

80

78 The swanshot link ledger. This is a handy bottom fishing rig, as weight can easily be added or subtracted, and the shot will slide off if caught in a snag.

79 If a weight of more than 6 or 7 swanshot is required, the paternoster link shown in this picture is the best rig to use.

80 Folding seat and tackle all ready for a barbel session.

81

81 Casting ledger tackle.

82 Here the ledger is dropped carefully into a gravel run.

83 84 85

83 A vital operation, too often forgotten — testing the clutch to see that a running fish can just pull off the line.

84 The overhead cast for float tackle.

85 Release the line at the right moment.

86

87

88

86 Great accuracy can be achieved.

87 Rod position as the float starts its journey. A finger on the spool controls the line.

88 Now the rod is lowered to keep contact with the float. A finger on the spool still controls the line.

89

90

91

89 'Mending' line, to keep it straight from rod tip to float.

90 Stret-pegging; the float is set over depth, and held back to work the bait under weed beds, etc.

91 Here the landing net can be seen ready to hand, stuck into the gravel, while a maggot container is fixed to a bank stick.

92

93

92 Retrieving float tackle out of the swim.

Playing and Landing

93 How to play your hooked barbel — controlling a short, powerful run.

94 Rod position after the first runs have been controlled.

96

95 Pumping — lowering and raising the rod while turning the reel handle to regain the line.

96 The tired barbel breaks surface, almost ready for the net.

97

98

99

97 The landing net must now be sunk ready for netting.

98 Bring the fish over the net: don't jab the net at the fish.

99 Lift the net until the barbel is well inside . . .

100

101

102

100 . . . Then release the pick-up and put down the rod carefully . . .

101 . . . Get both hands on the net handle.

102 Now draw in the net handle, not allowing it to bend too much . . .

103

103. . . Lift the net with one hand on each side of the rim.

104 How NOT to use a landing net. The hands are too far back on the handle so that the heavy weight of the fish will bend it and possibly break it.

105 Removing the hook with artery forceps.

104

105

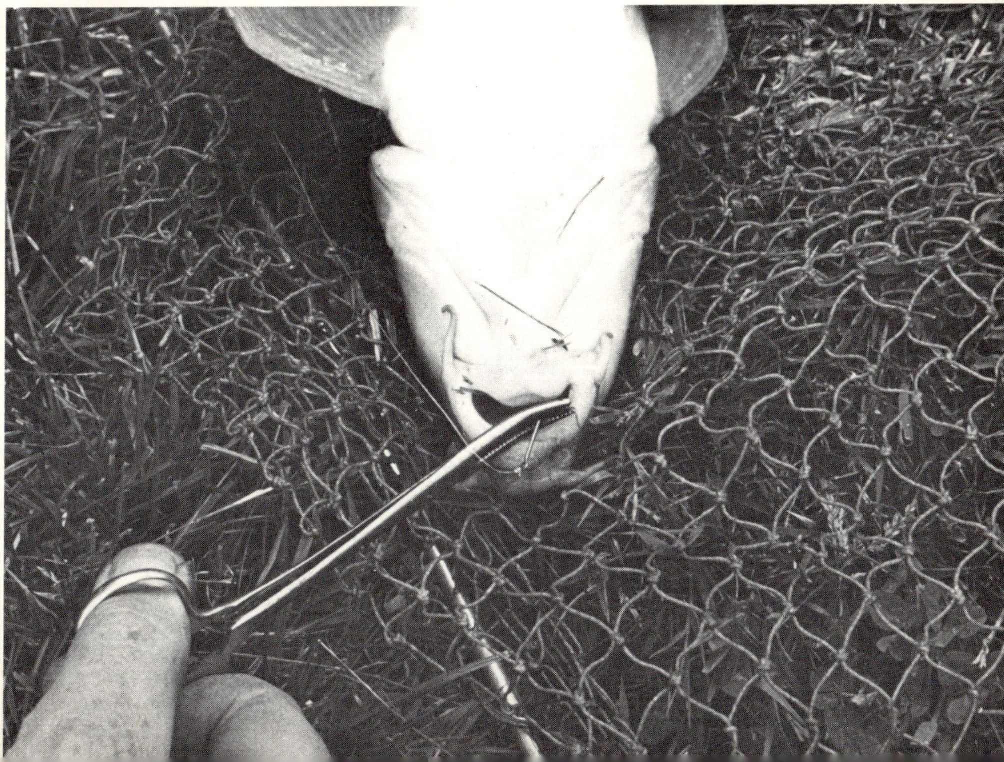

106

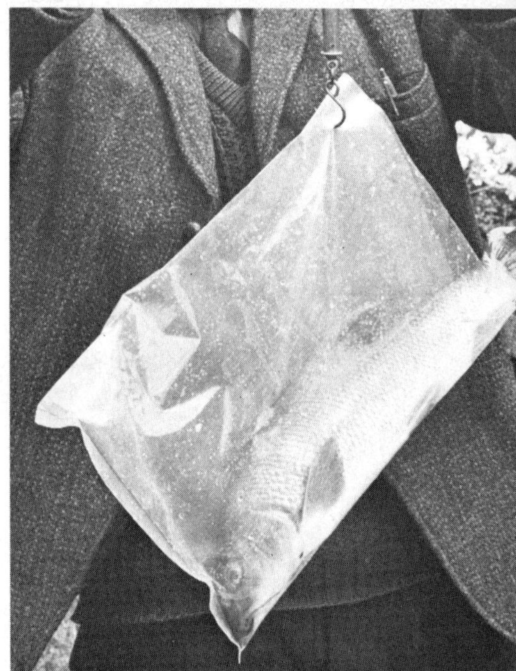

107

106 A nice barbel, ready for weighing.

107 Weigh the fish in a strong plastic bag to prevent damage. Heavier fish can be weighed in a laundry bag or in the landing net — not forgetting to subtract the weight of the net from the total!

108 Return the barbel carefully . . .

109 . . . Support it upright in the water until it swims away.

108

109

110

110 Unless allowed to recover in this way a tired fish can be swept away by the current, and may die.

Useful hints

111 Large keepnet pegged 'horizontally' in slack water in the correct manner.

112 Never hang the keepnet vertically in fast water as shown in this picture; it may cause split fins and damaged fish.

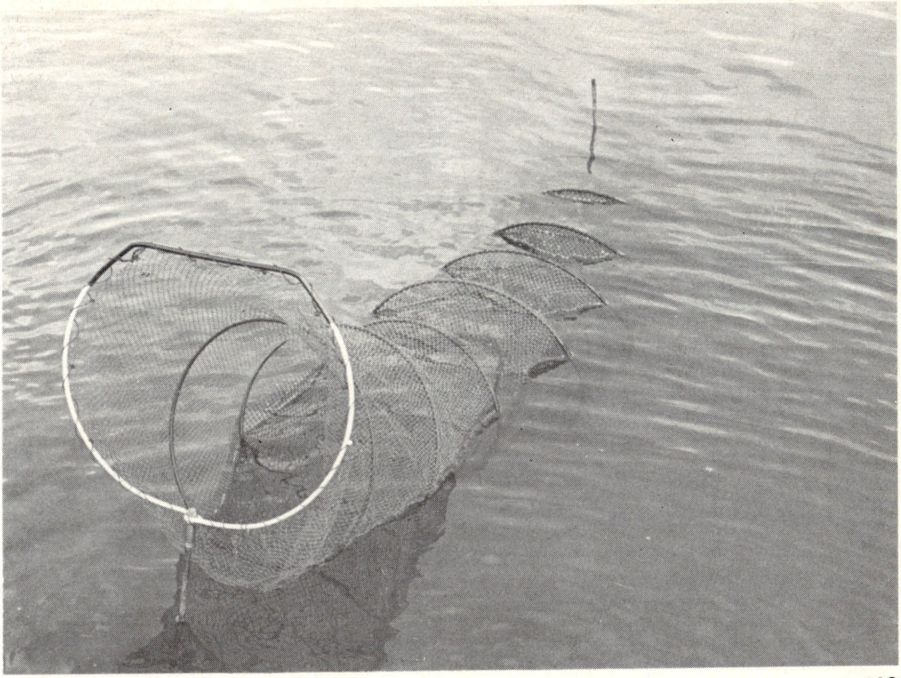

111

112

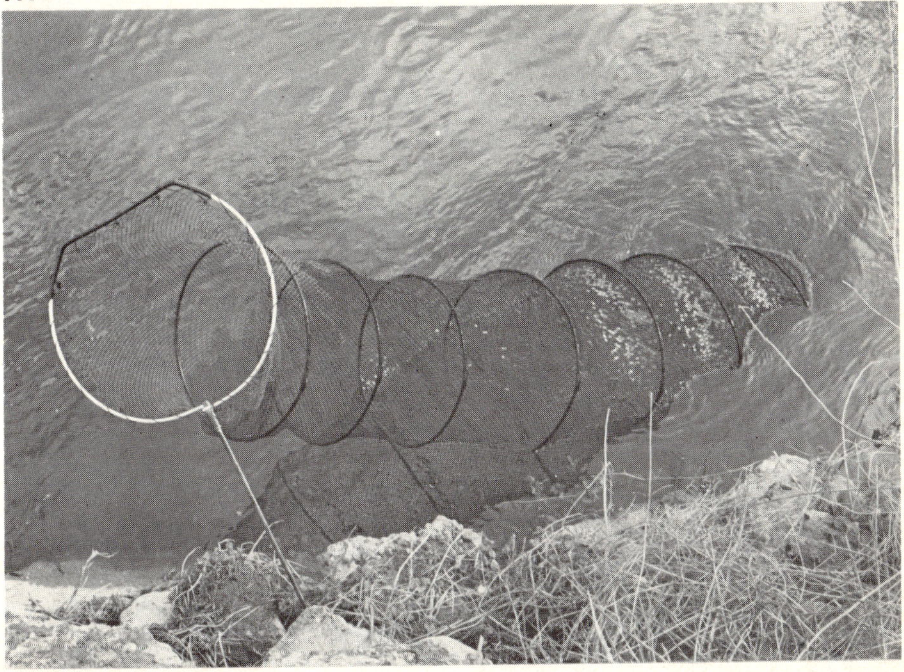

113

114

113 A hooked barbel is immovable in streamer weed. Don't keep pulling . . .

114 . . . Walk downstream, keeping the line taut.

115 Now pull on the fish from below, and it will usually come out of the weed easily.

The pictures you have seen show how an expert tackles Barbel fishing. Now go back to the beginning of the book and carefully study each sequence again. Compare the expert's approach with your own, and select what you think will improve your own fishing. Practise your new ideas — and then try to improve on them.

Always remember that an expert is the angler who constantly analyses his own styles, improves on what he is doing — and then practises until he is perfect.